T0414028

WOMEN IN STEM
KATHERINE JOHNSON
BARRIER-BREAKING MATHEMATICIAN

by Clara MacCarald

po go

Ideas for Parents and Teachers

Pogo Books let children practice reading informational text while introducing them to nonfiction features such as headings, labels, sidebars, maps, and diagrams, as well as a table of contents, glossary, and index.

Carefully leveled text with a strong photo match offers early fluent readers the support they need to succeed.

Before Reading

- "Walk" through the book and point out the various nonfiction features. Ask the student what purpose each feature serves.
- Look at the glossary together. Read and discuss the words.

Read the Book

- Have the child read the book independently.
- Invite him or her to list questions that arise from reading.

After Reading

- Discuss the child's questions. Talk about how he or she might find answers to those questions.
- Prompt the child to think more. Ask: Did you know about Katherine Johnson before reading this book? What more would you like to learn about her life or work?

Pogo Books are published by Jump!
5357 Penn Avenue South
Minneapolis, MN 55419
www.jumplibrary.com

Library of Congress Cataloging-in-Publication Data

Names: MacCarald, Clara, 1979- author.
Title: Katherine Johnson: barrier-breaking mathematician / by Clara MacCarald.
Description: Minneapolis, MN: Jump!, Inc., [2024]
Series: Women in STEM | Includes index.
Audience: Ages 7-10
Identifiers: LCCN 2023037037 (print)
LCCN 2023037038 (ebook)
ISBN 9798889967040 (hardcover)
ISBN 9798889967057 (paperback)
ISBN 9798889967064 (ebook)
Subjects: LCSH: Johnson, Katherine G. –Juvenile literature. | African American women mathematicians–Biography–Juvenile literature. | Mathematicians–United States–Biography–Juvenile literature. | United States. National Aeronautics and Space Administration–Officials and employees–Biography–Juvenile literature.
Classification: LCC QA29.J64 M33 2024 (print)
LCC QA29.J64 (ebook)
DDC 510.92 [B] –dc23/eng/20230824
LC record available at https://lccn.loc.gov/2023037037
LC ebook record available at https://lccn.loc.gov/2023037038

Editor: Katie Chanez
Designer: Emma Almgren-Bersie

Photo Credits: Bob Nye/NASA, cover (foreground), 1, 4, 19; NASA, cover (rocket), 8, 12, 12-13, 14-15, 16-17; Shutterstock, cover (background); Claudio Divizia/Shutterstock, 3; Glasshouse Images/Alamy, 5; UA-Visions/Shutterstock, 6-7; Science History Images/Alamy, 9; Florence_sketch/Shutterstock, 10-11; Dima Zel/Shutterstock, 18; Kris Connor/WireImage/Getty, 20-21; Africa Studio/Shutterstock, 23.

Printed in the United States of America at Corporate Graphics in North Mankato, Minnesota.

TABLE OF CONTENTS

CHAPTER 1

A MIND FOR NUMBERS

Katherine Johnson loved math. She was very good with numbers. She did tough **calculations**. She helped put **astronauts** on the Moon!

Katherine was born in 1918. Her family lived in West Virginia. The state was **segregated**. Black and white kids went to different schools.

1930s classroom

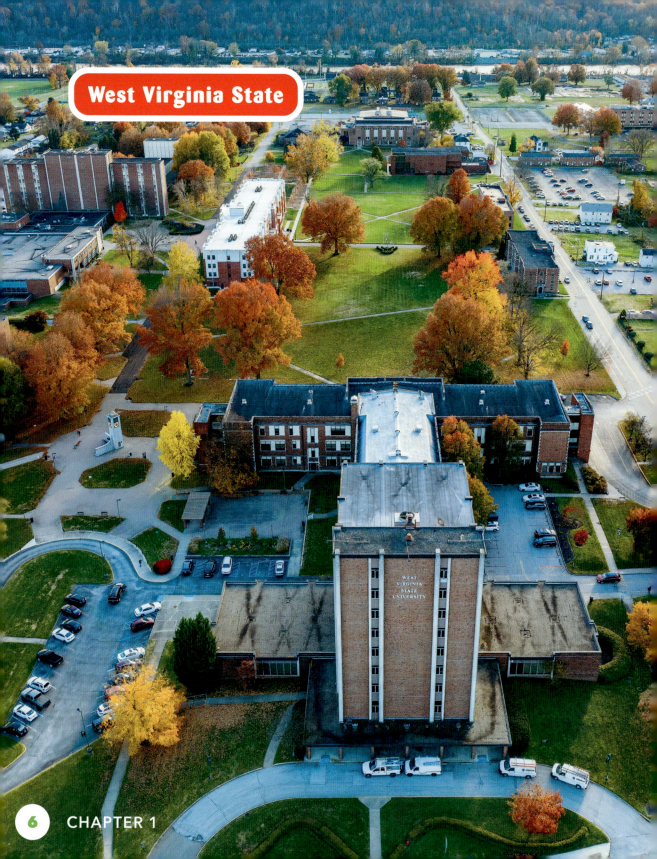

West Virginia State

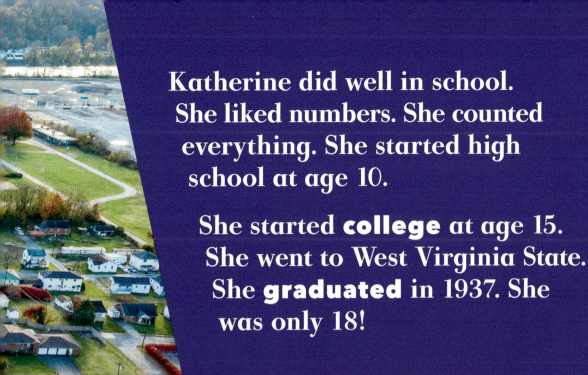

Katherine did well in school. She liked numbers. She counted everything. She started high school at age 10.

She started **college** at age 15. She went to West Virginia State. She **graduated** in 1937. She was only 18!

DID YOU KNOW?

Katherine went to **graduate school** after college. She was one of the first Black graduate students at her school.

CHAPTER 2

THE SPACE AGE

Katherine began working for a government **agency** in 1953. It would later be **NASA**. Many women already worked there. They used math to study airplanes and flight. They did math by hand. They were known as computers.

At the time, the agency was segregated. Black and white people worked in different areas. They could not eat together. They could not use the same bathrooms or drinking fountains.

In 1957, the **Soviet Union** sent a **satellite** into space. It was called Sputnik 1. The United States also wanted to explore space. Both countries wanted to send astronauts to space.

People at NASA respected Katherine. She asked big questions. She could do complicated math. NASA asked her to work on space flight.

DID YOU KNOW?

The United States and the Soviet Union competed. They both wanted to reach the Moon first. They both wanted to be first to send people to space. This was called the Space Race.

Sputnik I

Alan Shepard

John Glenn's launch

In 1961, Alan Shepard went to space. He was the first American to go. Katherine helped. How? She did calculations. She figured out how his **spacecraft** would get to space. She also figured out how it would land. Her math guided the flight.

John Glenn was an astronaut. In 1962, NASA used an electronic computer to find his **flight path**. John didn't trust the computer. He asked Katherine to check the math. John became the first American to **orbit** Earth.

In 1969, NASA set a new goal. The United States wanted to put astronauts on the Moon. NASA asked Katherine to help. She calculated a flight path.

Apollo 11 would orbit the Moon. A Moon lander would take astronauts to its surface. The lander had to return. Katherine figured out the lander's return path.

Apollo 11 launch

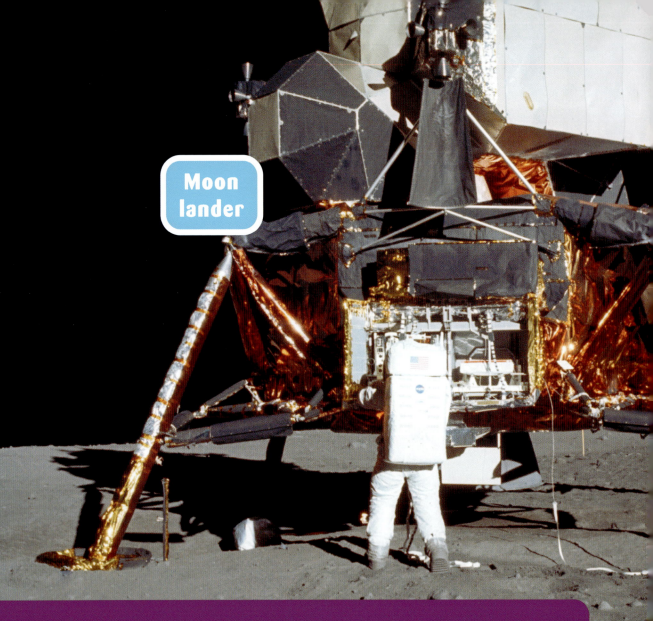

Moon
lander

Apollo 11 launched. It was July 16, 1969. Astronauts landed on the Moon on July 20. Millions watched on TV. But few knew how much Katherine did.

TAKE A LOOK!

How did Apollo 11 land astronauts on the Moon? Take a look!

1 Apollo 11 launched into outer space.

5 Apollo 11 returned to Earth.

2 It orbited the Moon.

4 The astronauts got back in the lander. It launched from the Moon. It met with Apollo 11.

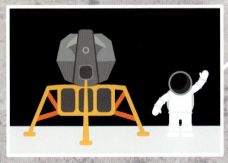

3 The Moon lander broke away. It brought astronauts to the Moon's surface. They stepped out. They walked on the Moon!

CHAPTER 3
HIDDEN FIGURE

Katherine worked on many NASA projects. She worked on satellites. They took pictures of Earth. She helped plan flights to Mars. She **retired** in 1986 after 33 years.

satellite

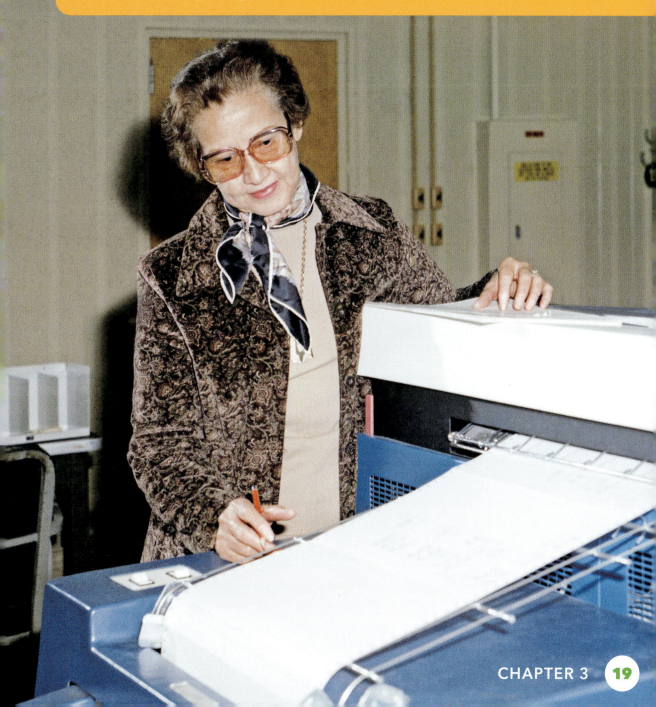

Katherine helped land people on the Moon. But most people did not know who she was.

Medal of Freedom

In 2015, President Barack Obama honored Katherine. How? He gave her the Presidential Medal of Freedom. It is one of the highest honors for an American.

Katherine died in 2020. She was 101. But she is remembered. She helped bring people to the Moon!

DID YOU KNOW?

In 2016, a movie called *Hidden Figures* came out. It was about Katherine and other Black women of NASA.

ACTIVITIES & TOOLS

LAUNCH A PAPER SPACECRAFT

Make a simple paper spacecraft to learn about different flight paths in this fun activity!

What You Need:
- ruler
- paper
- scissors
- straw
- tape

1. Cut a piece of paper that is about 1 inch (2.5 cm) wide and 5 inches (12.7 cm) long.

2. Wrap the paper around the straw to make a long tube. This is your spacecraft.

3. Tape the spacecraft to keep its shape. The tube of the spacecraft should be loose enough to move over the straw.

4. Take the craft off the straw. Squeeze one end of the paper to make a point. Tape the point closed so that no air comes through.

5. Cut three triangles out of the rest of the paper. These pieces should be shorter than the spacecraft. Tape these to the bottom of the spacecraft like a tail.

6. Place the spacecraft over the straw. Blow. See how the craft flies.

7. Launch from different angles. Does it change the flight path? How?

GLOSSARY

agency: A group that provides a service for the government.

astronauts: People trained to travel and work in space.

calculations: The processes of finding things out by using math.

college: A place that teaches higher learning beyond high school.

flight path: The journey an airplane or spacecraft takes through the air or space.

graduated: Successfully finished school or a grade level.

graduate school: A school for people who have graduated college and are continuing their studies.

NASA: The National Aeronautics and Space Administration; the United States' space agency.

orbit: To travel in a circular path around something.

retired: Stopped working, usually after reaching a certain age.

satellite: A spacecraft that is sent to orbit the Sun, Moon, or planets.

segregated: Separated or kept apart from the main group.

Soviet Union: A former country of 15 republics that included Russia, Ukraine, and other nations of eastern Europe and northern Asia.

spacecraft: Vehicles that travel in space.

INDEX

TO LEARN MORE

Finding more information is as easy as 1, 2, 3.

❶ Go to www.factsurfer.com

❷ Enter "KatherineJohnson" into the search box.

❸ Choose your book to see a list of websites.

FACT SURFER